D1196925

J. Michael Straczynski
Chris Roberson
WRITERS

Eddy Barrows
Allan Goldman
Travel Foreman
Diogenes Neves
Jamal Igle
PENCILLERS

J.P. Mayer
Eber Ferreira
Julio Ferreira
John Dell
Oclair Albert
Jon Sibal
Robin Riggs
INKERS

Marcelo Maiolo
Rod Reis
Dave McCaig
COLORISTS

John J. Hill
LETTERER

Jo Chen
COVER ARTIST

Superman created by Jerry Siegel and Joe Shuster

SUPERMAN GROUNDED

volume two

Matt Idelson Editor – Original Series / Wil Moss Associate Editor – Original Series
Ian Sattler Director – Editorial, Special Projects and Archival Editions / Peter Hamboussi – Editor / Robbin Brosterman Design Director – Books

Eddie Berganza Executive Editor / Bob Harras VP – Editor in Chief

Diane Nelson President / Dan DiDio and Jim Lee Co-Publishers / Geoff Johns Chief Creative Officer / John Rood Executive VP – Sales, Marketing and Business Development
Amy Genkins Senior VP – Business and Legal Affairs / Nairi Gardiner Senior VP – Finance / Jeff Boison VP – Publishing Operations / Mark Chiarello VP – Art Direction and Design
John Cunningham VP – Marketing / Terri Cunningham VP – Talent Relations and Services / Alison Gill Senior VP – Manufacturing and Operations / David Hyde VP – Publicity
Hank Kanalz Senior VP – Digital / Jay Kogan VP – Business and Legal Affairs, Publishing / Jack Mahan VP – Business Affairs, Talent
Nick Napolitano VP – Manufacturing Administration / Sue Pohja VP – Book Sales / Courtney Simmons Senior VP – Publicity / Bob Wayne Senior VP – Sales

SUPERMAN: GROUNDED, Volume 2
Published by DC Comics. Cover, text and compilation Copyright © 2011 DC Comics. All Rights Reserved. Originally published in single magazine form in
SUPERMAN 707-711, 713-714. Copyright © 2011 DC Comics. All Rights Reserved. All characters, their distinctive likenesses and related elements featured
in this publication are trademarks of DC Comics. DC Comics does not read or accept unsolicited ideas, stories or artwork.

DC Comics, 1700 Broadway, New York, NY 10019
A Warner Bros. Entertainment Company.
Printed by RR Donnelley, Salem, VA, USA. 11/04/11. First Printing.
ISBN: 978-1-4012-3316-7
SC ISBN: 978-1-4012-3532-1

DES MOINES, IOWA.

"IT'S BEEN A SLOW MORNING.

"SINCE REACHING TOWN, I'VE HELPED A POLICE OFFICER STOP A BANK ROBBERY...

"...KEPT A FREIGHT TRAIN FROM RUNNING OVER A LITTLE GIRL WHO RAN ONTO THE TRACK CHASING A LOST BALLOON...

"..AND STOPPED A MALFUNCTIONING HELICOPTER FROM CRASHING INTO THE TALLEST BUILDING IN IOWA..."

THIS SHOULD BE A BIG ENOUGH DOWNPOUR TO PUT OUT THE FLAMES.

I RAN INTO MANUEL HERE IN ST. LOUIS A FEW WEEKS AGO, TRYING TO GET SOMEONE IN THE E.P.A. TO LISTEN TO HIS STORY.

THEY *WOULDN'T*, BUT I *DID*, SO I CAME BACK WITH HIM TO KANSAS TO DO A PIECE FOR *THE DAILY PLANET*.

MANUEL USED TO WORK HERE AT THE CHEMICAL PLANT BUT LOST HIS JOB WHEN HE STARTED RAISING A STINK ABOUT THE LAX ENVIRONMENTAL STANDARDS.

THIS PLANT HAS BEEN IN OPERATION SINCE THE *FIFTIES*, AND IT'S STILL USING SIXTY-YEAR-OLD ENVIRONMENTAL PROTECTIONS.

WHENEVER NEW STANDARDS ARE PUT IN PLACE--

"--THE PLANT OWNERS JUST *BRIBE* THE INSPECTORS TO LET THEM KEEP USING THE *OLD* ONES RATHER THAN MAKE ANY *CHANGES.*

"THE POLLUTANTS THAT IT BELCHES INTO THE AIR ARE BAD ENOUGH.

"BUT THE *REAL* PROBLEM IS THE TOXIC WASTE LEAKING INTO THE GROUNDWATER.

"THE LEVEL OF CHLORIDE CONTAMINATION IN THE LOCAL AQUIFER HAS JUMPED 300% IN THE LAST TWO YEARS *ALONE.*"

I'VE TRIED TO BRING THE PROBLEM TO THE E.P.A., BUT THEY STAND BY THEIR LOCAL INSPECTORS. AND THE LOCAL INSPECTORS ARE *BOUGHT* AND *PAID* FOR.

I FIGURED A HIGH-PROFILE PIECE IN *THE PLANET* JUST MIGHT BE THE SOLUTION MANUEL'S BEEN LOOKING FOR.

I WAS ABOUT TO FILE MY STORY WHEN THE WHOLE PLANT WENT *KABLOOEY*. I GUESS THERE'S MORE STORY HERE THAN I *REALIZED*.

I LOOK FORWARD TO READING IT, MISS LANE. NOW IF YOU'LL EXCUSE ME, I'LL BE...

WAIT A MINUTE, SUPERMAN!

THESE ARE ALL JUST UNFOUNDED ALLEGATIONS! HE DOESN'T HAVE ANY *REAL* PROOF, AND...

ONLY BECAUSE *YOU* WON'T LET ANYONE DO AN INDEPENDENT SITE SURVEY!

IT SHOULD BE EASY ENOUGH TO CHECK.

LOOKS LIKE YOU'RE RIGHT, MANUEL. THERE *ARE* ELEVATED LEVELS OF CHLORIDE IN THE GROUNDWATER.

OKAY, OKAY, SO MAYBE THERE **ARE.**

BUT IT'S... IT'S **COMPLICATED.**

PROFIT MARGINS AT THIS PLANT HAVE NEVER BEEN GREAT, AND WITH THE ECONOMY THE WAY IT'S BEEN, WELL...

DO YOU HAVE ANY IDEA WHAT FULL ENVIRONMENTAL COMPLIANCE WOULD **COST**?

THAT'S NOT MUCH OF AN EXCUSE, SIR.

UM, SUPERMAN? I, UM...

I JUST WANTED TO SAY, WE **NEED** THIS PLANT. THE WHOLE **TOWN** DOES.

"THIS IS THE ONLY MAJOR EMPLOYER IN TOWN, EVER SINCE LEXCORP SHUT DOWN THE AIRCRAFT FACTORY AND SHIPPED THE JOBS OVERSEAS.

"NEARLY EVERYONE AROUND THESE PARTS WORKS RIGHT HERE, OR MAKES THEIR LIVING SELLING GOODS AND SERVICES **WE** BUY.

"IT'S A **GOOD** PLACE TO WORK. THE HOURS ARE DECENT, AND THE PAY IS GOOD.

"MY DADDY WORKED HERE, AND HIS BEFORE HIM."

FROM WHAT I'VE HEARD, CHLORIDE ISN'T EXACTLY *GOOD* FOR THE ENVIRONMENT, BUT IT ISN'T KILLING ANYBODY EITHER.

BUT--

THERE *MAY* BE SOME DAMAGE DONE TO PLANTS AND WILDLIFE IN THE LONG RUN, BUT THE HUMAN COST IS VIRTUALLY NIL.

WELL, NOT COUNTING THIS *EXPLOSION*...

HOW ABOUT THE REST OF YOU? IS THAT HOW YOU *ALL* FEEL?

YEP.

I FEEL BAD FOR THEM FISHES, BUT I'VE GOT A *FAMILY* TO FEED.

PLEASE DON'T LET THEM SHUT US DOWN, SUPERMAN.

YOU CAN'T *SERIOUSLY* BE CONSIDERING THIS, CAN YOU?

I DON'T KNOW, IT'S NOT ALL BLACK AND WHITE.

"THERE MAY BE A RIGHT AND A WRONG IN THIS UNIVERSE, LOIS...

"...BUT IT ISN'T ALWAYS EASY TO TELL THE DIFFERENCE."

THAT'S RIGHT, SUPERMAN.

THAT'S IT EXACTLY.

HE'S JUST LIKE THE *REST* OF THEM, MISS LANE. BOUGHT AND *PAID* FOR.

NOT NOW, MANUEL. JUST... NOT NOW.

IF I DIDN'T KNOW BETTER, I'D SWEAR THAT YOU REALLY HAD BEEN TURNED *EVIL* AGAIN BY RED KRYPTONITE...

NOT EVIL. JUST *REALISTIC*.

YEAH, *YOU* MIGHT NOT SHUT US DOWN, BUT IF THAT STORY GETS OUT, THEN THE AUTHORITIES ARE *SURE* TO.

THEY'RE RIGHT, MISS LANE.

WHAT ABOUT THE LADY REPORTER, SUPERMAN? WHAT ABOUT THE STORY SHE'S WRITING FOR THAT NEWSPAPER?

I'M AFRAID YOU *CAN'T* RUN THAT STORY.

GROUNDED
PART SIX

J. MICHAEL STRACZYNSKI plot CHRIS ROBERSON script

EDDY BARROWS penciller J.P. MAYER w/ JULIO FERREIRA inkers ROD REIS colorist JOHN J. HILL letterer

JOHN CASSADAY & DAVID BARON cover TREVOR HAIRSINE & VAL STAPLES variant cover

WIL MOSS associate editor MATT IDELSON editor SUPERMAN created by JERRY SIEGEL & JOE SHUSTER WONDER WOMAN created by WILLIAM MOULTON MARSTON

THIS...THIS IS *AMAZING*. WHAT *IS* THIS PLACE?

WELCOME TO THE HOME OF THE *SUPERMAN SQUAD*, THE MEN AND WOMEN OF *TOMORROW!*

THE FORTRESS IS A TESSERACT HOUSED IN A PENTAGONAL ICOSITETRAHEDRON OUTSIDE OF SPACE AND TIME, IN A REGION THAT SOME CULTURES HAVE TERMED "THE STILL ZONE."

FROM HERE, WE CAN EASILY REACH ANY POINT IN SPACETIME, FROM THE BIG *HAND* TO THE *END OF TIME.*

KAL KENT, THE SUPERMAN OF THE 853RD CENTURY, ONCE TOLD ME ABOUT YOUR "SUPERMAN SQUAD."

HE DESCRIBED IT AS A GROUP OF SUPERMEN FROM VARIOUS ERAS WHO'VE BANDED TOGETHER TO DEFEND THE TIME STREAM.

THAT'S IT EXACTLY. AND EACH AND EVERY ONE OF US IS HERE BECAUSE OF *YOU*. SOME ARE YOUR DESCENDANTS, ONE WAY OR ANOTHER.

OTHERS, LIKE *C.K.* AND *RA-BAK* HERE, HAVE BEEN ADOPTED INTO YOUR FAMILY, OR SHARE YOUR KRYPTONIAN HERITAGE.

BUT MANY ARE LIKE *MING*, HERE. SHE SHARES *NO* DIRECT CONNECTION WITH YOUR LEGACY, BUT WHEN SHE GAINED POWERS, SHE WAS INSPIRED BY YOUR EXAMPLE TO TAKE UP THE SHIELD.

THAT.

HURT.

GOOD. IT WAS **MEANT** TO.

WHO **ARE** YOU? SOME **LACKEY** OF THE CORPORATION? A **LAPDOG** OF THE MORRIGAN?*

WHO I AM IS NONE OF YOUR CONCERN. WHAT **DOES** MATTER--

--IS THAT YOU ARE MEDDLING IN **MY** BUSINESS.

THIS **SHOULD** HAVE BEEN AN **IMPOSSIBLE** CHOICE FOR SUPERMAN.

SHOULD HE SACRIFICE THE FEW FOR THE SAKE OF THE MANY? BUT THANKS TO YOU, HE NEVER HAD TO **DECIDE**.

I WON'T ALLOW YOU TO INTERFERE WITH MY PLANS EVER **AGAIN**.

I DON'T LIKE BEING **THREATENED!**

KRACK

*SEE WONDER WOMAN: ODYSSEY VOL. 1

COLORADO.

THANKS FOR YOUR HELP WITH THOSE TWO, SUPERMAN.

HEY, *YOU* CHASED THEM ALL THIS WAY, I JUST KEPT THEM DISTRACTED UNTIL YOU CAUGHT UP.

ONLY FIFTEEN MINUTES OF POWER LEFT UNTIL THE MANITOU STONE RUNS OUT OF JUICE FOR THE DAY, SO I SHOULD BE GETTING BACK.

YOU KNOW, I WAS TALKING TO A SCIENTIST FRIEND OF MINE, AND HE THINKS MAYBE THE MANITOU STONE IS KRYPTONIAN IN ORIGIN.

AS FAR AS I KNOW, ROCKS FROM KRYPTON ONLY TAKE POWERS *AWAY*, THEY DON'T *GRANT* THEM.

THIS IS MY FIRST REAL TEAM-UP. I MEAN, I'VE WORKED WITH MAN-OF-BATS A FEW TIMES, BUT THAT ALWAYS FELT SO...*CLICHÉ*, YOU KNOW?

WELL, IT'S BEEN A PLEASURE WORKING WITH YOU, SAGANOWAHNA.

PLEASE, CALL ME "SUPER-CHIEF." COMING FROM YOU, IT'S AN *HONOR*.

YOU'RE A METROPOLIS GUY, RIGHT? NEXT TIME THE METEORS PLAY GREEN BAY, YOU SHOULD COME TO TOWN-- WE'LL CATCH THE GAME.

SURE, THAT COULD BE FUN.

OKAY, I'LL SEE YOU LATER, SUPERMAN. GO PACKERS!

LATER...

LOIS, I--

--UNAVAILABLE TO TAKE YOUR CALL. LEAVE A MESSAGE AT THE TONE.

BEEP

IT'S ME AGAIN. I HAVEN'T HEARD BACK FROM YOU IN A WHILE, AND I THOUGHT I'D...

I *MISS* YOU, LOIS. I MISS THE SOUND OF YOUR VOICE.

GROUNDED
PART SEVEN

J. MICHAEL STRACZYNSKI & **CHRIS ROBERSON** writers

EDDY BARROWS & **ALLAN GOLDMAN** pencillers

J.P. MAYER & **JULIO FERREIRA** inkers

ROD REIS colorist **JOHN J. HILL** letterer

JOHN CASSADAY & **DAVID BARON** cover

KENNETH ROCAFORT variant cover

WIL MOSS associate editor **MATT IDELSON** editor

SUPERMAN created by **JERRY SIEGEL** & **JOE SHUSTER**

ROCKETED TO EARTH FROM THE DOOMED PLANET KRYPTON, THE BABY KAL-EL WAS FOUND AND RAISED BY JONATHAN AND MARTHA KENT IN SMALLVILLE, KANSAS. NOW AN ADULT, CLARK KENT CROSSES THE UNITED STATES LOOKING TO REDISCOVER TRUTH, JUSTICE & THE AMERICAN WAY AS...

SUPERMAN

SOMETHING... OR SOME*ONE*...IS DISGUISING THIS STREET TO LOOK LIKE A SCENE FROM ANCIENT KRYPTON. ALL WHILE QUOTING KRYPTONIAN HISTORY AT HYPERSPEED.

OR MAYBE *DISGUISING* ISN'T THE RIGHT WORD, BUT *COSTUMING.*

IT SEEMS MORE LIKE A HIGH SCHOOL THEATRICAL PRODUCTION THAN A HISTORICAL RE-CREATION.

⟨THE CLASSICAL WRITER BUR-EL...⟩

LOOKS LIKE THE SCENE IS CHANGING AGAIN. AND THAT VOICE IS ONTO A NEW QUOTATION.

⟨...WHO IN HIS "DIALOGUES OF KIL-GOR" RECORDED HIS MENTOR'S ASSERTION THAT "RIGHT AND WRONG ARE NATURAL ATTRIBUTES, LIKE HEAVY AND LIGHT...⟩

⟨"...MORALITY IS NOT THE ENEMY OF REASON; IT IS REASON'S CROWN."⟩

TAKING INTO ACCOUNT THE RATE OF DOPPLER SHIFT, I *SHOULD* BE ABLE TO TRIANGULATE THE *SOURCE* OF THAT VOICE.

FLASH! WAIT!

⟨...EROK-EL NAMED HIS FIRSTBORN SON "STAR-CHILD," OR KAL-EL...⟩

⟨...SINCE THE TIME OF RIK-AR, THE SYMBOL OF A FREE MAN OF KRYPTON HAS BEEN THE HEADBAND...⟩

ALMOST... THERE...

CLOSE, BUT NOT CLOSE ENOUGH.

GOTCHA!

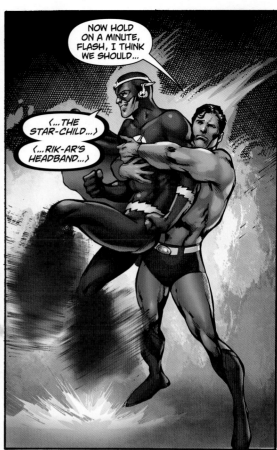

NOW HOLD ON A MINUTE, FLASH, I THINK WE SHOULD...

〈...THE STAR-CHILD...〉

〈...RIK-AR'S HEADBAND...〉

〈...STUDENTS INSTRUCTED BY THOUGHT TRANS-FERENCE...〉

OF COURSE.

I TAKE IT *THIS* IS THE SOURCE OF THE PROBLEM?

THANKS, SUPERMAN. I THOUGHT YOU'D *NEVER* WORK IT OUT.

THIS CRYSTAL, SET ON THE FRONT OF THE HEADBAND? IT'S KRYPTONIAN SUNSTONE.

THE LATTICE STRUCTURE RESEMBLES AN INTERROGATION DEVICE I ONCE SAW ON NEW KRYPTON THAT COULD EXTRACT MEMORIES DIRECTLY FROM A PRISONER'S MIND.

SOUNDS ABOUT RIGHT. EXCEPT THIS ONE APPEARS TO BE DESIGNED TO PUT MEMORIES *INTO* SOMEONE'S MIND.

BUT IT *CLEARLY* WASN'T INTENDED TO BE USED BY ANYONE BUT A *KRYPTONIAN*.

"I FOUND IT OUT IN THE SONORA DESERT, ON MY WAY BACK TO CENTRAL CITY FROM AUSTRALIA.

"FROM THE SIZE OF THE IMPACT CRATER, IT CAME DOWN WITH A LOT OF FORCE, BUT THERE DIDN'T APPEAR TO BE A SCRATCH ON IT.

"WHEN I SAW THAT IT WAS INTENDED TO BE WORN ON THE HEAD, I COULDN'T RESIST TRYING IT OUT. I GUESS YOU CAN BLAME THE SCIENTIST IN ME.

"BUT AS SOON AS I HAD IT ON, I WAS JUST OVERWHELMED BY THE FLOOD OF IMAGERY AND INFORMATION."

I FOUND I COULDN'T TURN IT *OFF*, AND THAT IT ALL BUT CROWDED OUT MY OWN *THOUGHTS*.

IT WAS *REALLY* CONFUSING FOR THE FIRST SIXTY OR SEVENTY SECONDS--

--BUT BY THEN I HAD TAUGHT MYSELF THE LANGUAGE AND REALIZED THAT IT WAS *KRYPTONIAN*.

"IT WAS WHEN I WAS STILL IN HIGH SCHOOL, BEFORE THE WORLD HAD EVER HEARD OF *SUPERMAN.*

"I WAS IN DETENTION, OF ALL PLACES. SOMEWHERE I DIDN'T SPEND A LOT OF TIME, NORMALLY.

"I DIDN'T MIND. GAVE ME TIME TO READ MY FAVORITE COMICS.

IRONMUNRO

"AND I *HAD* DONE WHAT I WAS BEING PUNISHED FOR. MORE OR LESS. IN ANY CASE, I WAS ALL ALONE IN THE DETENTION HALL, UNTIL *ANOTHER* STUDENT SHOWED UP."

NOW, MR. LUTHOR, MAYBE A LITTLE TIME IN *DETENTION* WILL HELP YOU REMEMBER WHERE YOU *PUT* THEM.

HMPH.

WHEN I GET *BACK,* I HOPE TO FIND YOU A LITTLE MORE *AGREEABLE.*

AND MR. KENT, NO FUNNY BOOKS ALLOWED. YOU KNOW BETTER THAN THAT.

"I'D TALKED WITH HIM A COUPLE OF TIMES BEFORE, BUT WE HAD NEVER REALLY BEEN FRIENDS.

"I LATER FOUND OUT THAT HE WAS THERE FOR STEALING FORTY CAKES FROM THE SCHOOL'S BAKE SALE."

"IT WAS HIS REVENGE ON A SCHOOL ADMINISTRATION THAT REFUSED TO LET HIM ENTER A FISSION-POWERED TOASTER IN THE SCIENCE FAIR."

AND WHAT ARE *YOU* DOING IN HERE?

I GOT CAUGHT SKIPPING CLASS. I MEAN, THEY *SAID* I WAS SKIPPING CLASS.

I WOULDN'T HAVE GOTTEN DETENTION IF I TOLD THEM I WAS REALLY...

WELL, I WASN'T IN CLASS LIKE I WAS SUPPOSED TO BE, ANYWAY, AND THAT'S WHAT MATTERS.

LET ME GET THIS STRAIGHT. YOU WEREN'T *REALLY* "SKIPPING" CLASS--PRESUMABLY BECAUSE YOU HAD SOME GOOD EXCUSE--AND YOU COULD HAVE ESCAPED PUNISHMENT SIMPLY BY *TELLING* THEM?

WHY *DIDN'T* YOU? IS THERE SOMETHING *WRONG* WITH YOU?

I DON'T KNOW, IT JUST DIDN'T SEEM *RIGHT*. IT'S LIKE MY DAD ALWAYS SAYS, "THERE IS RIGHT AND WRONG IN THIS UNIVERSE, AND THE DISTINCTION ISN'T HARD TO MAKE."

RIGHT AND *WRONG*?! THAT'S *RIDICULOUS*. THEY'RE *FAIRY TALES*.

THE ONLY *REAL* DISTINCTION IS BETWEEN WHAT *WORKS* AND WHAT *DOESN'T*.

YOU CAN STAY AND BE PUNISHED FOR A CRIME YOU DIDN'T COMMIT IF YOU LIKE, BUT *I* WON'T SPEND ANOTHER *SECOND* BEING PUNISHED FOR A CRIME I *DID*.

"AND THAT'S WHEN I UNDERSTOOD THAT WHAT HE WAS TALKING ABOUT WAS *PRAGMATISM*. ABOUT WHAT'S *EXPEDIENT*, INSTEAD OF WHAT'S *TRUE*."

BESIDES, I COULDN'T TELL MY TEACHERS THAT I SLIPPED OUT OF CLASS TO PUT OUT A FIRE THAT WAS RAGING IN A NEIGHBORING COUNTY.

THEY'D NEVER HAVE BELIEVED ME, ANYWAY.

I KNOW WHAT YOU MEAN. AS A SCIENTIST, I WAS TRAINED TO DISTRUST MORAL ABSOLUTES.

BUT MY EXPERIENCE HAS SHOWN ME THAT RIGHT AND WRONG *DO* EXIST.

AND I'VE GOT THE SCIENCE TO *PROVE* IT.

I'LL GET THIS.

WON'T HAVE TO CLEAN OUT ANY STORAGE ROOMS *THIS* TIME...

OOOH... HUH?

THANKS, MISS. THE PIE WAS *WONDERFUL*.

--RACE IS STILL UNDECIDED, THOUGH THE ODDS ARE WITH--

I STILL SAY KID FLASH WINS THIS, HANDS DOWN. HE'LL DO HIS GRANDFATHER PROUD.

EVEN IF I *DON'T* FEEL OLD ENOUGH TO HAVE A GRANDSON. OR EVEN A *SON*, FOR THAT MATTER.

SUPERBOY ISN'T EXACTLY MY "SON," BUT I KNOW WHAT YOU MEAN.

FAMILY GETS COMPLICATED WHEN YOU SPEND AS MUCH TIME AWAY AS I HAVE--IN THE TIME STREAM, THE SPEED FORCE, WHAT HAVE YOU--

BUT IT'S NICE TO KNOW THAT I'M LEAVING A LEGACY BEHIND.

I WAS MEANING TO ASK YOU ABOUT THAT. I'VE ONLY RECENTLY COME TO REALIZE THE EXTENT OF THE LEGACY *I* MIGHT LEAVE BEHIND.

DO YOU EVER WONDER IF YOU'RE DOING THE RIGHT THING? SETTING A COURSE THAT SO MANY OTHERS WILL FOLLOW?

IT WAS A LITTLE OVERWHELMING AT FIRST, I'LL ADMIT. I WAS THE *ONLY* FLASH WHEN I GOT STARTED. BUT THEN JAY CAME OUT OF RETIREMENT, AND WALLY CAME ALONG...

AND ALL OF THE TIMES I'VE BEEN AWAY, THERE'S ALWAYS BEEN A SPEEDSTER WILLING TO WEAR THE LIGHTNING AND FIGHT FOR JUSTICE AS *THE FLASH.*

NOW IT'S SOMETHING I TAKE COMFORT IN. IT'S AN *ABSOLUTE TRUTH* I CAN BELIEVE IN.

WHATEVER HAPPENS TO ME, THERE WILL *ALWAYS* BE A FLASH.

FROM WHAT I'VE SEEN OF THE FUTURE, YOU'LL LEAVE BEHIND QUITE A LEGACY OF YOUR OWN.

YOU SHOULD BE PROUD OF THE FACT THAT YOU'VE INSPIRED SO MANY OTHERS TO WEAR YOUR SHIELD-- SUPERBOY, SUPERGIRL, STEEL...

...AND PROUD OF THAT FACT THAT WHAT YOU DO IN THE HERE AND NOW WILL INSPIRE OTHERS TO FOLLOW IN YOUR FOOTSTEPS, SO THAT THIS WORLD WILL *ALWAYS* HAVE A PROTECTOR.

FLASH, I...THERE WAS SOMETHING *ELSE* I WANTED TO ASK.

WHEN I SAW YOU LAST, I ASKED WHAT YOU *SAW* WHEN YOU RAN CROSS-COUNTRY. AND YOU SAID YOU ONLY SAW A *BLUR.*

I SAID--? WAIT, ARE YOU *SERIOUS*?

I WAS *JOKING!* I THOUGHT YOU *KNEW* THAT.

I CAN THINK AT THE SPEED OF *LIGHT*, I CAN PERCEIVE EVENTS THAT LAST FOR LESS THAN AN *ATTOSECOND*, I CAN RUN FASTER THAN *TIME*.

WHAT DO I SEE WHEN I RUN ACROSS THE COUNTRY, SUPERMAN? I SEE *EVERYTHING*. AND *EVERYONE*.

THANKS, FLASH. I...WELL, I'VE BEEN A LITTLE *DEPRESSED* LATELY, AND I'M TOLD THAT MY PERCEPTIONS MIGHT HAVE GOTTEN A LITTLE...SKEWED.

FROM WHAT I UNDERSTAND, YOU RECENTLY LOST YOUR ADOPTIVE FATHER, AND THEN YOU LOST A WHOLE *PLANET*.

THAT WOULD TAKE *ANYONE* SOME TIME TO BOUNCE BACK FROM, EVEN A SUPERMAN.

I'VE HAD MY DARK DAYS, TOO, AND I CAN TELL YOU, IT *DOES* GET BETTER. MIGHT NOT SEEM THAT WAY TO YOU RIGHT NOW, BUT IT *DOES*.

JUST REMEMBER, THOUGH, I *LET* YOU CATCH ME TODAY. I'M *STILL* THE FASTEST MAN ALIVE!

OGDEN, UTAH.

"I DIDN'T KNOW WHO SHE WAS, OR WHY SHE WAS YELLING AT THE MAN ACROSS THE STREET..."

DON'T WALK AWAY FROM ME--!

"...BUT IT WAS CLEAR THAT SHE DIDN'T NOTICE THE TRUCK BARRELING TOWARDS HER."

UNNNNGH.

"SHE ALMOST FAINTED WHEN SHE REALIZED HOW CLOSE SHE'D COME TO A SERIOUS ACCIDENT."

ARE YOU ALL RIGHT, MA'AM? IS THERE SOMEWHERE I CAN TAKE YOU? HOME? THE HOSPITAL?

I--I JUST NEED TO REST. I HAVE A TRAILER JUST OUTSIDE OF TOWN, AND--

THEN LET ME GIVE YOU A LIFT.

"OF COURSE, WHEN SHE SAID 'JUST OUTSIDE OF TOWN,' I HAD NO IDEA SHE MEANT ALMOST 80 MILES."

"AS WE FLEW OVER THE GREAT SALT LAKE AND INTO SKULL VALLEY, SHE INTRODUCED HERSELF AS DR. HELEN PHELPS, ARCHAEOLOGIST."

"BUT EVEN IF SHE *HADN'T* TOLD ME, I'D SPENT ENOUGH TIME ON DIGS WITH PROFESSOR LANG TO RECOGNIZE AN ARCHAEOLOGICAL SITE WHEN I SEE ONE."

OVER THIS WAY, SUPERMAN, I'LL SHOW YOU WHAT BROUGHT US HERE TO MT. KROWAK.

THE RANCHER WHO OWNED THIS LAND WAS DIGGING A WELL WHEN HE TURNED UP SOME RATHER *UNUSUAL* BITS OF POTTERY AND SCULPTURE.

HE THOUGHT THEY WERE GOSHUTE PIECES, MAYBE SHOSHONE. THE SCHOOLTEACHER HE SHOWED THEM TO KNEW ENOUGH TO CALL *US*.

TO BE HONEST, WE'RE NOT SURE *WHO* MADE THEM. WE'VE FOUND DOZENS OF PIECES, ALL OF THEM SHOWING CONSIDERABLE SOPHISTICATION.

AND FROM ALL INDICATIONS, THESE PIECES DATE BACK TO *BEFORE* PALEO-INDIANS SETTLED HERE.

THIS COULD REWRITE THE HISTORY OF HUMAN SETTLEMENT IN THIS REGION.

THAT IS, UNTIL CENTUM INDUSTRIES PURCHASED THIS PROPERTY TO USE AS A RADIOACTIVE *WASTE* SITE. THEY'VE ORDERED US OFF THE MOUNTAIN, BY THE END OF THE WEEK.

"SHE EXPLAINED THAT THE MAN SHE'D BEEN CHASING IN OGDEN WAS CENTUM INDUSTRIES' LOCAL REPRESENTATIVE--

"--BUT THAT'S WHEN I SPOTTED SOMETHING IN THE SKY."

WHAT IS IT? ALL I SEE IS *CLOUDS*.

"I HADN'T YET MOVED TO METROPOLIS AND STARTED MY CAREER AS SUPERMAN, AND WAS STILL TRAVELING THE WORLD, HELPING PEOPLE IN SECRET.

"I WAS IN AFRICA WHEN I GOT TERRI'S MESSAGE ASKING ME TO RETURN TO BHUTRAN. WE'D BEEN IN LOVE ONCE UPON A TIME, BEFORE HER NEW JOB CAME BETWEEN US."*

"I WAS STILL STUDYING, BUT I FELT LIKE I WAS NEARLY READY TO RETURN TO GOTHAM, THAT I'D ALMOST LEARNED ENOUGH TO DO WHAT NEEDED TO BE DONE.

"I'D BEEN DOWN IN THE ARABIAN PENINSULA, AND WHEN I GOT THE SUMMONS, I ASSUMED IT WAS FROM THE OLD RHANA BHUTRAN, MY FORMER TEACHER.

*SEE THE SUPERMAN : THE ODYSSEY ONE-SHOT.
--HOMERIC MATT

"UNTIL I MET YOU ON THE STEPS, I DIDN'T REALIZE ANYONE ELSE HAD BEEN CALLED IN."

YOU DON'T LOOK BHUTRANESE.

"I'D FIRST COME TO BHUTRAN A YEAR OR SO BEFORE WITH TERRI CHUNG, THE DAUGHTER OF THEIR LEADER, THE RHANA BHUTRAN."

"I WAS SURPRISED TO LEARN THAT THE OLD MAN HAD DIED, AND THAT HIS DAUGHTER HAD BECOME THE NEW RHANA BHUTRAN AFTER HIS DEATH."

"I WASN'T SURE WHETHER HER FATHER HAD TOLD HER EVERYTHING ABOUT ME, OR IF SHE'D BE HAPPY TO SEE ME IF HE HAD. YOU, CLEARLY, HAD NOTHING TO WORRY ABOUT."

IT IS SO GOOD TO SEE YOU!

AND THANK YOU FOR COMING, TOO. MY FATHER ALWAYS SPOKE HIGHLY OF YOU.

I... THAT IS...WELL, HOW COULD I REFUSE THE CALL OF THE RHANA BHUTRAN?

TERRI...ERM, YOUR HOLINESS, I MEAN... YOUR MESSAGE SAID SOMETHING ABOUT A THREAT?

YES, THERE IS AN ARMY MASSED AT OUR BORDER. THEIR GENERAL BELIEVES THAT WE KNOW THE SECRET WAY TO NANDA PARBAT, AND IS THREATENING TO INVADE UNLESS WE SHARE IT WITH HIM.

IS HE RIGHT? DO YOU KNOW THE WAY TO NANDA PARBAT?

WHO IS THIS GENERAL?

I'M NOT CERTAIN. HIS MEN KNOW HIM ONLY AS SHENG FAN.

"I KNEW ENOUGH CHINESE TO KNOW WHAT THE NAME MEANT: CANNIBAL..."

"...OR SAVAGE.

"THIS WOULD BE MY FIRST TIME ENCOUNTERING THE UNDYING CAVEMAN, VANDAL SAVAGE... THOUGH NOT HIS FIRST TIME ENCOUNTERING ME, I'VE SINCE DISCOVERED.

"BUT THE EXPLOSION 50,000 YEARS AGO THAT HAD TURNED HIM IMMORTAL HAD AFFECTED ALL OF HIS CELLS, EVEN THE CANCEROUS CELLS OF THE TUMORS IN HIS GUT.

"THE CANCER COULD NEVER KILL HIM, BUT AT TIMES THE PAIN MADE HIM WISH HE WAS DEAD."

"MY FRIEND SIROCCO LATER EXPLAINED THAT VANDAL HAD LEARNED OF NANDA PARBAT FROM ANOTHER IMMORTAL, HASSAN-I-SABBAH.

"IN EXCHANGE FOR CYBERNETIC UPGRADES FOR HIS GHOST WOLVES, THE ASSASSIN LORD TOLD VANDAL THAT THE MONKS OF RAMA KUSHNA MIGHT BE ABLE TO TAKE AWAY HIS PAIN.

"HASSAN-I-SABBAH ONLY KNEW OF NANDA PARBAT'S EXISTENCE, NOT WHERE IT COULD BE FOUND. BUT HE BELIEVED THAT THOSE IN BHUTRAN KNEW THE SECRET.

"SO VANDAL CORRUPTED AN ENTIRE BATTALION OF THE CHINESE RED ARMY, LURING THEM AWAY FROM THEIR DUTIES TO FIGHT FOR HIM IN EXCHANGE FOR POWER AND RICHES.

"IT WAS CLEAR WE HAD VERY DIFFERENT IDEAS ABOUT WHAT *JUSTICE* IS, BUT WE WERE TOO BUSY PREPARING BHUTRAN'S DEFENSES TO DEBATE THE MATTER."

"TERRI ASSURED ME THAT YOU WERE SWORN TO SECRECY ABOUT MY... STRENGTHS, BUT EVEN SO, I WAITED UNTIL I WAS ALONE TO START BLOCKING THE MOUNTAIN PASSES."

"IT WASN'T ALL THAT DIFFERENT FROM CLEARING THE FIELDS ON MY PARENTS FARM, REALLY."

"AND WHILE I KNEW I COULD FIGHT ANY MAN--ANY *DOZEN* MEN--EVEN MY SKILL WITH MARTIAL ARTS WASN'T ENOUGH TO STOP AN *ARMY.*"

"AND WHEN EVERYTHING WAS READY, ALL WE COULD DO WAS *WAIT.*"

"I MUST ADMIT, I ENVIED HOW EASILY YOU RELATED TO CHILDREN, AND DOUBTED I COULD EVER BE SO COMFORTABLE AROUND THEM."

"IF WE WERE GOING TO DEFEAT THE INVADERS, WE WOULD HAVE TO USE PSYCHOLOGY. USE *FEAR* AS A WEAPON. SO I FOUND THE MOST *FRIGHTENING* THING I COULD THINK OF."

"WE DIDN'T HAVE TO WAIT *LONG*."

‹YOU *WILL* TELL ME THE WAY TO NANDA PARBAT.›

‹I SHALL SQUEEZE THE INFORMATION FROM YOUR BODY ALONG WITH YOUR *LIFEBLOOD*, IF I MUST.›

"BUT WHEN THE TIME CAME, WE WERE *READY*."

‹I CANNOT DO THAT, SHENG FAN. AND WOULD NOT, IF I COULD. YOU THINK YOU CAN *INTIMIDATE* US, SIMPLY BECAUSE THE PEOPLE OF BHUTRAN ARE DEDICATED TO *PEACE*.›

‹BUT JUST BECAUSE THIS IS NOT A HOME FOR WARRIORS DOES NOT MEAN THAT WE DO NOT COUNT WARRIORS AMONG OUR *FRIENDS*.›

"I HAD BEEN HELPING PEOPLE ALOT OVER THE YEARS, BUT ALWAYS IN SECRET, AT SUPER-SPEED, WITHOUT ANYONE NOTICING."

"I'D FOUGHT CRIMINALS COUNTLESS TIMES IN MY TRAVELS AROUND THE WORLD, BUT NEVER SUCH A LARGE AND ORGANIZED FORCE."

"OPERATING OUT IN THE OPEN LIKE THAT, NOT HIDING WHO AND WHAT I WAS, IT FELT...IT FELT RIGHT."

"BEFORE THAT DAY, I'D ALWAYS CONSIDERED CRIME-FIGHTING A ONE-MAN OPERATION. BUT SUDDENLY I COULD SEE THE ADVANTAGE OF WORKING WITH A PARTNER."

WELL, SHE'S NOT THERE *NOW.* I WAS IN TOWN WORKING ON A STORY ABOUT THE GORILLA MOB MOVING INTO VEGAS, WHEN *SHE* SHOWED UP.

SHE TOOK A BUNCH OF HOSTAGES, AND SAYS SHE'LL *FRY* THEM UNLESS THE CITY GIVES HER-- GET THIS--*ALL* OF THE MONEY IN TOWN.

AND YOU SAY SHE'S HOLDING THEM INSIDE THE G.B.S. GRANDE?

"THERE THEY ARE, ALL RIGHT.

"SHE'S GOT THEM PENNED IN WITH *RINGS* OF LIGHTNING."

BUT HOW IS SHE *DOING* THIS? LIVEWIRE'S NEVER HAD *THIS* KIND OF CONTROL BEFORE.

MAYBE SHE PICKED UP A FEW POINTERS AT S.T.A.R.?

SOMEHOW I DOUBT IT. BUT EITHER WAY, I'M HERE TO PUT A *STOP* TO THIS.

HERE, KEEP AN EYE ON THIS, WILL YOU?

WHAT'S THAT?

...OLSEN, AND I'M TRYING TO REACH DR. SERLING ROQUETTE?

THAT'S THINKING, JIMMY.

DR. ROQUETTE? I HEARD YOU WERE AT S.T.A.R. LABS NOW, AND WAS WONDERING, WERE YOU ONE OF THE RESEARCHERS WHO WORKED WITH LIVEWIRE?

SHE IS *WAY* MORE POWERFUL THAN BEFORE, BUT SHE'S ACTING *CRAZY*, AND...

OH, *POOP*, I WAS *AFRAID* SOMETHING LIKE THIS WOULD HAPPEN.

LESLIE IS CAPABLE OF TRANSFORMING INTO *PURE* ENERGY. SHE CAN *DISCHARGE* IT, *ABSORB* IT, YOU NAME IT.

BUT AS A RESULT, HER ENERGY LEVELS ARE CONSTANTLY *FLUCTUATING*, AND WHEN YOU CONSIDER THAT HER *BRAIN* IS PART OF THAT ENERGY MIX, WELL...

THE ONLY WAY TO KEEP HER FROM GOING ALL *LOOPY* WOULD BE TO USE SOME KIND OF *CONTAINMENT* SUIT THAT COULD REGULATE HER BODY'S ENERGY.

"I DON'T KNOW WHERE YOU'D FIND ONE OF *THOSE* LYING AROUND, THOUGH..."

THAT SHOULD DO THE TRICK.

I'VE MADE A DECISION, AND IT AFFECTS THE BOTH OF YOU.

ROCKETED TO EARTH FROM THE DOOMED PLANET KRYPTON, THE BABY KAL-EL WAS FOUND AND RAISED BY JONATHAN AND MARTHA KENT IN SMALLVILLE, KANSAS. NOW AN ADULT, CLARK KENT CROSSES THE UNITED STATES LOOKING TO REDISCOVER TRUTH, JUSTICE & THE AMERICAN WAY AS...

SUPERMAN

J. MICHAEL STRACZYNSKI & CHRIS ROBERSON writers
DIOGENES NEVES & OCLAIR ALBERT (pgs. 1, 4-10) EDDY BARROWS & JP MAYER (pgs. 2-3)
JAMAL IGLE & JON SIBAL (pgs. 11-20) artists MARCELO MAIOLO colorist JOHN J. HILL letterer
JOHN CASSADAY & DAVID BARON cover JEFF SMITH variant cover
WIL MOSS associate editor MATT IDELSON editor SUPERMAN created by JERRY SIEGEL & JOE SHUSTER

YOU'VE DECIDED TO KEEP WALKING UNTIL YOU HIT METROPOLIS FROM THE OTHER SIDE?

SERIOUSLY, KAL, WE'RE WORRIED ABOUT YOU. IT SEEMS LIKE THIS CROSS-COUNTRY TRIP HAS BEEN YOU RUNNING AWAY FROM SOMETHING.

I HAVEN'T BEEN RUNNING AWAY, KARA. I'VE BEEN SEARCHING FOR AN ANSWER TO A QUESTION: "MUST THERE BE A SUPERMAN?"

AND THE ANSWER, I'VE REALIZED, IS "NO."

IT WAS MORE IMPORTANT TO SUPERMAN TO TELL US A HARSH BUT NECESSARY *TRUTH* THAN IT WAS TO GO WITH A COMFORTING *LIE.*

I COULDN'T AGREE MORE, MA'AM. AND THANKS FOR YOUR TIME.

OKAY, FAIR POINT. THERE *ARE* PEOPLE WHO *DON'T* FEAR SUPERMAN, OR DISTRUST OR RESENT HIM.

BUT THAT DOESN'T MEAN *EVERYONE* FEELS THE SAME WAY.

LOOK, THE ONLY PEOPLE WHO ARE *AFRAID* OF SUPERMAN, I THINK, ARE PEOPLE WHO'VE DONE SOMETHING *WRONG.*

BUT EVEN *THEY* KNOW SUPERMAN'S NOT GOING TO *HURT* THEM.

EXCUSE ME, SIR?

DO YOU THINK THAT SUPERMAN *HARMS* OR EVEN *KILLS* THE VILLAINS HE CAPTURES?

SUPERMAN? KILL A DUDE? NO *WAY.*

I MEAN, I DON'T KNOW IF *I'D* BE ABLE TO HOLD BACK, DEALING WITH A GUY WHO WANTED TO MURDER *KIDS*.

BUT I GUESS IF *I* WAS THE ONE ACCUSED OF A CRIME, I'D WANT A *COURT* TO DECIDE IF I WAS GUILTY OR INNOCENT, AND NOT SOME *GUY*, SUPER OR *NOT*. WOULDN'T *YOU*?

OKAY, OKAY. SO SUPERMAN *DOES* STAND FOR SOME THINGS THAT PEOPLE BELIEVE IN.

BUT DOESN'T THE FACT THAT HE HAS POWERS AND THEY *DON'T* MAKE THEM *RESENT* HIM?

I DON'T KNOW, LET'S FIND OUT.

EXCUSE ME, FOLKS. WE'RE DOING A QUICK SURVEY, AND I WAS WONDERING IF WE COULD ASK YOU A QUESTION.

DO YOU *RESENT* THE FACT THAT SUPERMAN HAS *SUPERPOWERS* AND YOU *DON'T*?

SUPERMAN! HE'S MY *FAVORITE*!

RESENT HIM? WE THANK HEAVEN EVERY *DAY* THAT HE CAN DO THINGS WE *CANNOT* DO.

HE SAVED *BUBBLES*! HE'S MY *HERO*!

IT DIDN'T MATTER TO SUPERMAN THAT MY HUSBAND AND I WERE NOT BORN IN THIS COUNTRY, EITHER. HE HELPS *EVERYONE* WHO NEEDS HIM. THAT'S THE *AMERICAN WAY*.

SEEMS TO ME I'VE HEARD THAT SOMEWHERE BEFORE. TELLING THE TRUTH, SEEING JUSTICE DONE, ENSURING LIFE, LIBERTY, AND THE PURSUIT OF HAPPINESS FOR ALL.

TRUTH, JUSTICE, AND THE AMERICAN WAY. NOT A BAD LINEUP, IF YOU ASK ME.

MY WIFE SAID MUCH THE SAME THING, NOT LONG AGO.

SHE'S A BIG FAN OF SUPERMAN'S, TOO.

I KNOW WHO YOUR WIFE IS, MR. KENT. I READ THE PAPERS, AFTER ALL.

AND IF YOU ASK ME, *SHE'S* THE ONE WHO KNOWS MORE ABOUT SUPERMAN THAN ANYONE ELSE.

I'M BEGINNING TO THINK MAYBE YOU'RE RIGHT ABOUT *THAT*.

--THE SCENE JUST MOMENTS AGO IN SEATTLE, WHERE A SUPERPOWERED WOMAN HAS BEGUN TO ISSUE DEMANDS.

THE IDENTITY OF THE WOMAN IS UNKNOWN, BUT HER HOSTAGE *HAS* BEEN POSITIVELY IDENTIFIED AS DAILY PLANET REPORTER LOIS LANE.

LOIS?!

AND THAT *WOMAN* WITH HER! IT'S GOT TO BE THE ONE WHO'S BEEN *FOLLOWING* ME!

WE NOW RETURN LIVE TO THE SCENE AS EVENTS UNFOLD.

--YOU HEAR ME, SUPERMAN? SHOW YOURSELF, OR I WILL *KILL* LOIS LANE!

WJLA

YOU SHOULD BE SAFE HERE, LOIS.

SORRY I DIDN'T MAKE IT SOONER, BUT I HAD TO *CHANGE*.

REDMOND
BICYCLE CAPITAL OF THE NORTHWEST

LOOK, I KNOW WE DON'T HAVE TIME TO *TALK*, BUT I WANT YOU TO KNOW...

THERE'S A *LOT* I NEED TO SAY TO YOU-- A LOT I NEED YOU TO *HEAR*--

--BUT FIRST, I HAVE TO DEAL WITH THIS *WOMAN*, WHOEVER SHE IS.

BE CAREFUL, SMALLVILLE.

FWOOOSH

MY NAME IS LISA JENNINGS. I TEACH HIGH SCHOOL SCIENCE IN DANVILLE, OHIO.

AT LEAST THAT'S WHO I *WAS* UNTIL I TOUCHED *THIS*!

A KRYPTONIAN SUNSTONE?! AN *INTERROGATION* DEVICE?

TWO OF MY STUDENTS FOUND IT IN A FIELD. THEY THOUGHT IT WAS A METEORITE, AND BROUGHT IT TO ME.

"BUT *YOU* WERE PASSING BY JUST THEN, IN THE MIDDLE OF YOUR 'SAD SUPERMAN WALK' ACROSS AMERICA.

"AND WHEN I TOUCHED THE SUNSTONE JUST AS YOU PASSED BY A FEW YARDS AWAY...

"MY HEAD WAS SUDDENLY *FILLED* WITH ALL OF THESE *THOUGHTS* AND *FEELINGS*. WITH ALL OF *YOUR* THOUGHTS AND FEELINGS, SUPERMAN.

"ALL OF YOUR GRIEF, AND YOUR *SADNESS*, AND YOUR *DOUBT*..."

...IT ALL CAME POURING INTO *MY* MIND!

IT *FILLED* MY *HEAD*!

"AND SUPERMAN *DID* RETURN HOME TO METROPOLIS, BUT NOT BEFORE MAKING A FEW STOPS ALONG THE WAY."

"IN GREEN BAY, WISCONSIN, HE GAVE A SIGNAL WATCH TO SAGANOWHANA, THE HERO BETTER KNOWN AS *SUPER-CHIEF.*"

"HE GAVE ANOTHER JUST LIKE IT TO HIS FRIEND JOHN HENRY IRONS--*STEEL*."

"SUPERMAN EXPLAINED THAT HE HAD LEARNED IN HIS WALK ACROSS AMERICA THAT HE COULD NOT BE EVERYWHERE AT *ONCE*."

"SUPERMAN HAD DECIDED TO CREATE A NETWORK OF HEROES HE COULD CALL UPON, SPREAD OUT ALL ACROSS THE MAP."

"HEROES LIKE HIS CHILDHOOD INSPIRATION *IRON MUNRO*, AND THE NOW REFORMED *LIVEWIRE.*"

"AND IN SMALLVILLE, *SUPERBOY* AND *SUPERGIRL* WERE HAPPY TO HEAR THAT HE HAD DECIDED AGAINST RETIRING THE CAPE AND SHIELD."

"THEY ACCEPTED THE SIGNAL WATCHES, LIKE ALL OF THE OTHERS, AND PROMISED TO ANSWER WHENEVER SUPERMAN CALLED."

THE FORTRESS OF SOLIDARITY, THE STILL ZONE.

AND IN CREATING THAT NETWORK OF HEROES--*THE SUPERMEN OF AMERICA*, AS IT CAME TO BE KNOWN--SUPERMAN FINALLY EMBRACED HIS LEGACY.

SO IF SUPERMAN HADN'T EMBRACED THAT LEGACY, THE *SUPERMAN SQUAD* WOULD NEVER HAVE EXISTED? WOW.

BUT WHAT HAPPENED TO THE KRYPTONIAN SUNSTONE?

THE SHARDS FOUND THEIR WAY BACK TO NORMAL SPACE, IN TIME.

"FRAGMENTS OF SUNSTONE FELL ON THE EARTH LIKE METEORS THROUGHOUT HISTORY. EACH CONTAINED THE ESSENCE OF SUPERMAN--HIS POWERS, HIS IDEALS."

"MANY HEROES AROSE OVER TIME, SHARING A PORTION OF SUPERMAN'S POWER WITHOUT EVER REALIZING ITS SOURCE."

WHAT ABOUT LISA JENNINGS? DID SHE GO BACK HOME?

DID SHE RETURN TO NORMAL AFTERWARDS?

SUPERMAN 711 Variant Cover
Dave Johnson

Unused Cover
by Geof Darrow with Peter Doherty